I0017338

Learn SAP Fieldglass: A Comprehensive Guide to Streamlining Workforce Management

Table of Contents:

Chapter 1: Introduction to SAP Fieldglass

Welcome to the first chapter of "Mastering SAP Fieldglass: A Comprehensive Guide to Streamlining Workforce Management." In this chapter, we will introduce you to SAP Fieldglass and provide you with a solid foundation of knowledge to kick-start your journey into mastering this powerful workforce management platform.

Section 1: Understanding SAP Fieldglass

What is SAP Fieldglass?

SAP Fieldglass is a cloud-based vendor management system (VMS) that helps organizations manage their contingent workforce and external service providers efficiently. It provides a centralized platform for managing all aspects of workforce procurement, from requisition creation to invoicing and payment.

Key Features and Benefits

Vendor and Supplier Management: SAP Fieldglass enables you to establish relationships with vendors, manage supplier profiles, and define contractual terms and agreements.

Requisition Management: With SAP Fieldglass, you can create and manage requisitions for contingent workers, ensuring a streamlined and efficient hiring process.

Contingent Worker Management: The platform allows you to onboard and offboard contingent workers, track worker assignments and profiles, and facilitate talent acquisition and retention.

Cost Control and Budgeting: SAP Fieldglass helps you manage budgets, track spend data, and optimize cost efficiency through comprehensive analytics.

Work Order and Deliverable Management: You can create work orders, define deliverables, and monitor project progress and milestones using SAP Fieldglass.

Reporting and Analytics: The platform offers robust reporting and analytics capabilities, allowing you to generate standard reports and customize them to meet your specific needs.

Evolution and Significance of SAP Fieldglass

SAP Fieldglass has evolved over the years to become a market-leading solution for workforce management. It offers organizations the ability to streamline their contingent workforce processes, enhance visibility and control, and drive greater operational efficiency.

The significance of SAP Fieldglass lies in its ability to bring together various stakeholders, including procurement, human resources, and hiring managers, onto a single platform. It enables seamless collaboration, reduces manual effort, and ensures compliance with labor laws and regulations.

Section 2: Getting Started with SAP Fieldglass

Now that you have an understanding of SAP Fieldglass and its key features, let's move on to getting started with the platform.

Setting up your SAP Fieldglass Account

To begin using SAP Fieldglass, you need to set up your account. Follow these steps:

Contact your organization's SAP Fieldglass administrator or IT department to obtain your login credentials.

Open your preferred web browser and navigate to the SAP Fieldglass login page.

Enter your username and password provided by your administrator.

Upon successful login, you will be directed to the SAP Fieldglass dashboard.

Navigating the SAP Fieldglass User Interface

The SAP Fieldglass user interface (UI) is designed to be intuitive and user-friendly. Here are some key elements you will encounter:

Navigation Menu: Located on the left side of the screen, the navigation menu provides access to different modules and functionalities within SAP Fieldglass.

Dashboard: The dashboard is the main landing page that displays an overview of your activities, pending tasks, and key metrics.

Tabs and Sections: Within each module, you will find tabs and sections that organize information and allow you to perform specific actions.

Search Functionality: The search bar at the top of the screen enables you to quickly find specific information or records.

Configuring Personal Preferences and Notifications

SAP Fieldglass allows you to personalize your experience by configuring your personal preferences and notifications. Here's how:

Click on your username or profile picture in the top-right corner of the screen.

Select "Preferences" from the dropdown menu.

In the preferences menu, you can customize various settings such as language, date format, and time zone to match your preferences.

Additionally, you can set up email notifications for specific events or actions within SAP Fieldglass to stay updated on important activities.

Congratulations! You have now completed the first chapter of "Mastering SAP Fieldglass." In this chapter, you learned the basics of SAP Fieldglass, including its definition, key features, and significance in workforce management. You also explored how to set up your account, navigate the user interface, and configure personal preferences.

In the next chapter, we will dive deeper into managing vendors and suppliers within SAP Fieldglass.

Chapter 2: Managing Vendors and Suppliers

Welcome to Chapter 2 of "Mastering SAP Fieldglass: A Comprehensive Guide to Streamlining Workforce Management." In this chapter, we will explore the process of managing vendors and suppliers within SAP Fieldglass. Effective vendor and supplier management is essential for successful workforce procurement and optimization.

Section 1: Adding and Managing Vendor Profiles

To effectively manage vendors and suppliers within SAP Fieldglass, it is crucial to have accurate and up-to-date vendor profiles. Here's how you can add and manage vendor profiles:

From the SAP Fieldglass dashboard, navigate to the "Vendors" section.

Click on the "Add New Vendor" button to create a new vendor profile.

Fill in the required information, such as vendor name, address, contact details, and any other relevant details.

Save the vendor profile, and it will be added to your list of vendors.

To manage existing vendor profiles, select the vendor from the list and click on the "Edit" button to make changes or updates as necessary.

Ensure that vendor profiles are regularly reviewed and updated to maintain accurate information.

Section 2: Establishing Relationships with Suppliers

SAP Fieldglass allows you to establish and maintain relationships with your suppliers. This helps streamline communication, negotiate contracts, and manage the overall supplier network. Follow these steps to manage supplier relationships:

Within the vendor profile, navigate to the "Suppliers" tab.

Click on the "Add Supplier" button to associate a supplier with the vendor.

Select the supplier from the available list or create a new supplier profile if needed.

Specify the relationship type, such as prime supplier or sub-supplier.

Enter any additional information or contractual agreements related to the supplier relationship.

Save the supplier association, and it will be linked to the vendor profile.

Repeat the process to establish relationships with other suppliers for the vendor if required.

Section 3: Defining Contractual Terms and Agreements

Clear and well-defined contractual terms and agreements are crucial for effective vendor management. SAP Fieldglass provides features to define and manage contracts within the system. Here's how you can do it:

Within the vendor profile, navigate to the "Contracts" tab.

Click on the "Add New Contract" button to create a new contract.

Fill in the required details, such as contract start and end dates, contract type, and any specific terms or conditions.

Attach any relevant documents or files related to the contract.

Save the contract, and it will be associated with the vendor profile.

Review and update contracts regularly to ensure compliance and to reflect any changes or renewals.

By effectively managing vendor profiles, establishing supplier relationships, and defining contractual terms and agreements, you can streamline the vendor and supplier management process within SAP Fieldglass. This enables you to have better control over your external workforce procurement and optimization.

In the next chapter, we will explore the creation and management of requisitions within SAP Fieldglass. Requisitions play a crucial role in the hiring process, and understanding their management is essential for effective workforce procurement.

Chapter 3: Creating and Managing Requisitions

Welcome to Chapter 3 of "Mastering SAP Fieldglass: A Comprehensive Guide to Streamlining Workforce Management." In this chapter, we will delve into the creation and management of requisitions within SAP Fieldglass. Requisitions are a fundamental part of the hiring process, serving as the foundation for procuring contingent workers and managing workforce needs.

Section 1: Understanding Requisitions and Their Role

Requisitions in SAP Fieldglass represent the demand for contingent workers or external service providers within your organization. They outline the requirements and specifications for the positions you seek to fill. Understanding the role of requisitions is crucial for effective workforce procurement. Here are the key aspects to consider:

Identifying Workforce Needs: Requisitions help identify and document the specific workforce needs within your organization, such as skill sets, experience requirements, and the number of workers needed.

Initiating the Hiring Process: Requisitions serve as the starting point for initiating the hiring process. They provide essential information that guides the entire procurement workflow.

Defining Job Descriptions and Requirements: Requisitions allow you to define detailed job descriptions, including responsibilities, qualifications, and any specific criteria for the positions.

Budgeting and Cost Control: Requisitions play a crucial role in budgeting and cost control. By outlining the desired contingent worker profiles and their associated costs, organizations can better manage their financial resources.

Section 2: Configuring and Customizing Requisition Templates

SAP Fieldglass provides the flexibility to configure and customize requisition templates according to your organization's specific needs. These templates serve as the basis for creating requisitions and ensure consistency across your workforce procurement process. Follow these steps to configure and customize requisition templates:

Access the requisition template management section within SAP Fieldglass.

Select the default template or create a new template based on your requirements.

Define the required fields and sections for the template, such as job title, department, skills, experience, and any other pertinent details.

Customize the template layout, including the order and grouping of fields, to align with your organization's preferred format.

Configure validation rules and default values for fields to ensure data integrity and streamline the requisition creation process.

Save the requisition template for future use.

Section 3: Managing Requisition Approvals and Workflows

Requisition approvals and workflows help streamline the hiring process and ensure appropriate authorization and compliance. SAP Fieldglass offers robust functionality to manage approvals and workflows. Here's how you can configure requisition approvals and workflows:

Define the approval hierarchy within SAP Fieldglass, specifying the individuals or roles responsible for approving requisitions at each level.

Configure approval rules based on criteria such as requisition value, department, or job type.

Determine the sequence and order of approvals, including any parallel or sequential approval paths.

Set up automatic notifications to inform approvers about pending requisitions requiring their attention.

Define escalation rules to ensure timely processing of requisitions and avoid bottlenecks.

Test and validate the requisition approval workflow to ensure it functions as intended.

By understanding the role of requisitions, configuring and customizing requisition templates, and effectively managing requisition approvals and workflows, you can streamline the hiring process and optimize workforce procurement within SAP Fieldglass.

In the next chapter, we will explore the management of contingent workers within the platform. Understanding how to onboard, track, and retain contingent workers is essential for effective workforce management.

Chapter 4: Managing Contingent Workers

Welcome to Chapter 4 of "Mastering SAP Fieldglass: A Comprehensive Guide to Streamlining Workforce Management." In this chapter, we will focus on the management of contingent workers within SAP Fieldglass. Contingent workers play a crucial role in workforce optimization, and efficient management is key to ensuring productivity and compliance.

Section 1: Onboarding and Offboarding Contingent Workers

The onboarding and offboarding process for contingent workers is essential to ensure a smooth transition into and out of your organization. SAP Fieldglass provides features to facilitate this process. Here's how you can manage onboarding and offboarding:

Onboarding:

Create a new worker profile within SAP Fieldglass, including personal details, job role, and any necessary documentation.

Assign appropriate access levels and permissions based on the worker's role and responsibilities.

Define the onboarding tasks and requirements, such as completing mandatory training or submitting necessary certifications.

Monitor the progress of onboarding tasks and ensure all requirements are fulfilled before the worker begins their assignment.

Offboarding:

Initiate the offboarding process for workers who have completed their assignments or are no longer required.

Collect any company assets or equipment from the worker, if applicable.

Conduct exit interviews or surveys to gather feedback and insights.

Update the worker's profile and status in SAP Fieldglass to reflect their offboarding.

Section 2: Tracking Worker Profiles and Assignments

SAP Fieldglass allows you to efficiently track and manage worker profiles and assignments, providing visibility into their details and statuses. Here's how you can effectively track worker profiles and assignments:

Worker Profiles:

Maintain accurate and up-to-date worker profiles in SAP Fieldglass, including personal information, qualifications, skills, and experience.

Regularly review and update worker profiles to ensure accuracy and reflect any changes or updates.

Worker Assignments:

Create assignments for contingent workers within SAP Fieldglass, specifying the project, location, duration, and other relevant details.

Track the progress of worker assignments, including start and end dates, deliverables, and milestones.

Monitor worker performance and compliance with contractual obligations.

Capture and document any changes or updates to assignments, such as extensions, amendments, or early terminations.

Worker Communication:

Utilize communication features within SAP Fieldglass to facilitate efficient and effective communication with workers, such as sharing important updates, providing feedback, or addressing any concerns.

Section 3: Leveraging SAP Fieldglass for Talent Acquisition and Retention

SAP Fieldglass offers functionalities that can help organizations in talent acquisition and retention efforts. Here's how you can leverage SAP Fieldglass for these purposes:

Talent Acquisition:

Utilize SAP Fieldglass to search and identify potential contingent workers based on criteria such as skills, qualifications, and availability.

Leverage the platform's analytics and reporting capabilities to gain insights into talent pools and make informed hiring decisions.

Streamline the sourcing and selection process by managing candidate profiles and evaluations within SAP Fieldglass.

Talent Retention:

Utilize performance evaluation features within SAP Fieldglass to assess worker performance and provide feedback for improvement.

Monitor worker satisfaction and engagement levels through surveys or feedback mechanisms integrated into the platform.

Leverage analytics and reporting to identify trends and opportunities for improving worker retention and engagement.

By effectively managing the onboarding and offboarding of contingent workers, tracking worker profiles and assignments, and leveraging SAP Fieldglass for talent acquisition and retention, you can optimize your workforce management efforts and ensure productivity and compliance.

In the next chapter, we will explore cost control and budgeting within SAP Fieldglass. Understanding how to manage budgets, track spend data, and optimize cost efficiency is crucial for effective workforce management and financial control.

Chapter 5: Controlling Costs and Budgeting

Welcome to Chapter 5 of "Mastering SAP Fieldglass: A Comprehensive Guide to Streamlining Workforce Management." In this chapter, we will dive into the important aspects of cost control and budgeting within SAP Fieldglass. Effective management of costs and budgets is essential for optimizing workforce procurement and ensuring financial control within your organization.

Section 1: Managing Budgets and Cost Centers

SAP Fieldglass provides features that allow you to manage budgets and cost centers, enabling better financial control and allocation of resources. Here's how you can effectively manage budgets and cost centers within the platform:

Budget Setup:

Define and set up budgets within SAP Fieldglass for specific projects, departments, or cost centers.

Allocate budget amounts based on the expected workforce needs and associated costs.

Specify the budget duration and any limitations or restrictions.

Budget Monitoring:

Track the actual spend against the allocated budgets within SAP Fieldglass.

Monitor the budget utilization in real-time to ensure compliance and avoid overspending.

Set up alerts or notifications for budget thresholds to proactively manage costs.

Cost Center Allocation:

Assign costs to specific cost centers within SAP Fieldglass to accurately track expenses and allocate them to the appropriate departments or projects.

Define cost center hierarchies and structures to align with your organization's financial reporting and analysis requirements.

Section 2: Monitoring and Analyzing Spend Data

SAP Fieldglass offers robust reporting and analytics capabilities that enable you to monitor and analyze spend data effectively. By leveraging these features, you can gain insights into your workforce procurement expenses and make informed decisions. Here's how you can monitor and analyze spend data within the platform:

Standard Reports and Dashboards:

Utilize the standard reports and dashboards provided by SAP Fieldglass to get an overview of spend data, including total expenses, cost breakdowns, and budget utilization.

Customize and filter these reports to focus on specific cost centers, projects, or time periods.

Custom Reports:

Create custom reports within SAP Fieldglass to analyze spend data based on your specific requirements.

Define the report parameters, data fields, and visualization options to generate tailored reports that provide deeper insights into your workforce procurement costs.

Data Export and Integration:

Export spend data from SAP Fieldglass for further analysis or integration with other financial management systems.

Leverage integration options to connect SAP Fieldglass with your organization's enterprise resource planning (ERP) system for seamless data exchange and consolidated financial reporting.

Section 3: Optimizing Cost Efficiency through SAP Fieldglass Analytics

SAP Fieldglass offers powerful analytics capabilities that can help optimize cost efficiency and drive informed decision-making. Here are some ways to leverage SAP Fieldglass analytics for cost optimization:

Cost Performance Analysis:

Analyze the cost performance of different vendors, suppliers, or projects within SAP Fieldglass to identify opportunities for cost savings or efficiency improvements.

Compare spend data across different time periods or cost centers to identify trends or anomalies.

Rate Benchmarking:

Utilize SAP Fieldglass analytics to benchmark rates and costs against industry standards or market averages.

Identify areas where rates can be renegotiated or optimized to achieve cost savings without compromising quality.

Contract Compliance Monitoring:

Monitor contract compliance through SAP Fieldglass analytics to ensure that costs align with agreed-upon terms and rates.

Identify instances of non-compliance or discrepancies to take appropriate action.

By effectively managing budgets and cost centers, monitoring and analyzing spend data, and leveraging SAP Fieldglass analytics, you can optimize cost efficiency, maintain financial control, and make informed decisions in your workforce management efforts.

In the next chapter, we will explore the management of work orders and deliverables within SAP Fieldglass. Work orders are an essential component of project-based workforce management, and understanding their management is crucial for successful execution.

Chapter 6: Managing Work Orders and Deliverables

Welcome to Chapter 6 of "Mastering SAP Fieldglass: A Comprehensive Guide to Streamlining Workforce Management." In this chapter, we will explore the management of work orders and deliverables within SAP Fieldglass. Effectively managing work orders and tracking deliverables is vital for successful project execution and ensuring quality control.

Section 1: Creating Work Orders and Defining Deliverables

Work orders serve as the foundation for project-based workforce management within SAP Fieldglass. They outline the specific tasks, requirements, and deliverables for each project. Here's how you can create work orders and define deliverables within the platform:

Work Order Creation:

Access the work order management section within SAP Fieldglass.

Create a new work order for each project or assignment, specifying the project details, scope, and timeline.

Define the tasks, milestones, and key deliverables associated with the work order.

Assign the appropriate contingent workers or service providers to the work order.

Deliverable Definition:

Within each work order, define the specific deliverables expected from the contingent workers or service providers.

Clearly outline the deliverable requirements, quality standards, and submission deadlines.

Provide any necessary guidelines, templates, or documentation for the deliverables.

Section 2: Tracking Project Progress and Milestones

SAP Fieldglass allows you to track the progress of work orders and monitor the achievement of project milestones. Here's how you can effectively track project progress and milestones within the platform:

Progress Tracking:

Regularly update the status and progress of work orders within SAP Fieldglass.

Provide updates on completed tasks, ongoing activities, and any challenges or issues encountered.

Utilize the platform's collaboration features to facilitate communication and collaboration among project stakeholders.

Milestone Monitoring:

Define project milestones within each work order, representing significant achievements or deadlines.

Monitor the completion of milestones and ensure they are met according to the project timeline.

Generate automated notifications or alerts for upcoming or missed milestones.

Quality Assurance:

Use SAP Fieldglass to enforce quality control measures for deliverables.

Establish review and approval processes to ensure that deliverables meet the defined standards and requirements.

Capture feedback and revisions within the platform to maintain a comprehensive audit trail.

Section 3: Ensuring Compliance and Quality Control

Compliance and quality control are critical aspects of workforce management. SAP Fieldglass provides features that help ensure compliance and maintain quality standards. Here's how you can ensure compliance and quality control within the platform:

Compliance Monitoring:

Define compliance requirements, such as certifications, background checks, or legal obligations, within work orders.

Monitor and track compliance status for each contingent worker or service provider.

Generate compliance reports to ensure adherence to relevant regulations or industry standards.

Audit Trails and Documentation:

Maintain detailed audit trails within SAP Fieldglass to document all activities, changes, and communications related to work orders and deliverables.

Attach supporting documentation, such as contracts, agreements, or certifications, to the respective work orders.

Ensure proper version control and accessibility of documents for auditing purposes.

Quality Control Measures:

Implement quality control measures for deliverables, such as peer reviews, quality assessments, or client approvals.

Utilize SAP Fieldglass analytics to identify potential quality issues or trends and take corrective actions.

By effectively creating work orders, defining deliverables, tracking project progress and milestones, and ensuring compliance and quality control, you can optimize project execution and deliver successful outcomes within SAP Fieldglass.

In the next chapter, we will explore the reporting and analytics capabilities of SAP Fieldglass. Understanding how to generate reports and leverage analytics is essential for gaining insights and making informed decisions in workforce management.

Chapter 7: Reporting and Analytics

Welcome to Chapter 7 of "Mastering SAP Fieldglass: A Comprehensive Guide to Streamlining Workforce Management." In this chapter, we will delve into the reporting and analytics capabilities of SAP Fieldglass. Effective reporting and analytics allow you to gain insights into your workforce data, monitor key metrics, and make data-driven decisions.

Section 1: Generating Standard Reports and Dashboards

SAP Fieldglass provides a range of standard reports and dashboards that offer valuable insights into your workforce management activities. Here's how you can generate standard reports and leverage dashboards:

Accessing Standard Reports:

Navigate to the reporting section within SAP Fieldglass.

Explore the library of pre-built standard reports available in the platform.

Selecting Relevant Reports:

Review the available reports and identify those that align with your reporting requirements.

Choose reports that provide insights into key areas such as spend analysis, worker performance, compliance, or vendor performance.

Configuring Report Parameters:

Customize report parameters, such as date range, cost center, project, or worker type, to focus the report on specific data subsets.

Specify the desired output format (e.g., PDF, Excel) and any additional filters or sorting options.

Generating Reports:

Click on the "Generate" or "Run" button to generate the report based on the defined parameters.

View, save, or export the generated report for further analysis or sharing.

Exploring Dashboards:

Navigate to the dashboard section within SAP Fieldglass.

Explore the pre-built dashboards that provide visual representations of key metrics and trends.

Customizing Dashboards:

Customize dashboards by selecting relevant widgets and arranging them according to your preferences.

Configure the data sources and filters for each widget to display the desired information.

Section 2: Customizing Reports to Meet Specific Needs

SAP Fieldglass allows you to customize reports to meet your specific reporting needs and requirements. Here's how you can customize reports within the platform:

Report Builder:

Access the report builder functionality within SAP Fieldglass.

Define the report structure, including data fields, filters, and sorting options.

Selecting Data Fields:

Choose the relevant data fields that you want to include in the report.

Customize the column headers, calculations, or aggregations as needed.

Applying Filters:

Apply filters to narrow down the data based on specific criteria, such as cost center, project, worker type, or date range.

Utilize advanced filter options for more complex filtering conditions.

Configuring Grouping and Sorting:

Configure grouping and sorting options to organize the report data in a meaningful way.

Group data based on criteria such as vendor, department, or project to facilitate analysis.

Saving and Sharing Custom Reports:

Save the customized report for future use or as a template for recurring reporting needs.

Share the report with relevant stakeholders, such as managers or executives, for review or decision-making.

Section 3: Utilizing Analytics to Gain Insights

SAP Fieldglass offers powerful analytics capabilities that enable you to gain deeper insights into your workforce management data. Here's how you can utilize analytics within the platform:

Analyzing Data Trends:

Utilize analytics features to identify trends and patterns within your workforce data.

Analyze key metrics such as spend trends, worker performance, or vendor performance over time.

Comparative Analysis:

Conduct comparative analysis by comparing data across different periods, projects, cost centers, or worker types.

Identify variations or anomalies and investigate underlying factors.

Forecasting and Predictive Analytics:

Leverage forecasting and predictive analytics capabilities within SAP Fieldglass to project future workforce needs, costs, or performance.

Utilize historical data and statistical models to make data-driven predictions and optimize workforce planning.

Interactive Visualizations:

Utilize interactive visualizations, such as charts, graphs, or heatmaps, to present complex data in a more intuitive and comprehensible manner.

Customize the visualizations to highlight specific insights or emphasize key metrics.

By effectively generating standard reports and leveraging dashboards, customizing reports to meet specific needs, and utilizing analytics to gain insights, you can leverage the power of SAP Fieldglass to make informed decisions, optimize workforce management strategies, and drive continuous improvement.

In the next chapter, we will explore the integration capabilities of SAP Fieldglass and how it can be seamlessly integrated with other systems to streamline data exchange and improve overall efficiency.

Chapter 8: Integrating SAP Fieldglass with Other Systems

Welcome to Chapter 8 of "Mastering SAP Fieldglass: A Comprehensive Guide to Streamlining Workforce Management." In this chapter, we will explore the integration capabilities of SAP Fieldglass and how it can be seamlessly integrated with other systems to streamline data exchange and improve overall efficiency. Integration plays a crucial role in connecting SAP Fieldglass with your organization's existing ecosystem and ensuring seamless flow of information.

Section 1: Exploring Integration Options with ERP Systems

Integrating SAP Fieldglass with your organization's Enterprise Resource Planning (ERP) system can enhance the overall efficiency of your workforce management processes. Here are some integration options to consider:

Data Synchronization:

Establish a data synchronization process between SAP Fieldglass and your ERP system to ensure the consistency and accuracy of data across both platforms.

Sync data such as vendor details, cost centers, project information, and worker profiles.

Purchase Order Integration:

Integrate SAP Fieldglass with your ERP system to automatically generate purchase orders based on approved requisitions.

Ensure that requisition details, such as job requirements, worker rates, and project information, are seamlessly transferred to the ERP system.

Invoice Integration:

Streamline the invoicing process by integrating SAP Fieldglass with your ERP system.

Automatically transfer approved time and expense data from SAP Fieldglass to the ERP system for accurate and timely invoicing.

Financial Integration:

Integrate SAP Fieldglass with your ERP system's financial module to consolidate financial data and streamline financial reporting.

Enable seamless flow of cost data, budget information, and payment details between the systems.

Section 2: Integrating with Other HR and Workforce Management Tools

In addition to ERP integration, SAP Fieldglass can be integrated with other Human Resources (HR) and workforce management tools to create a cohesive ecosystem. Here are some integration options to consider:

Applicant Tracking System (ATS) Integration:

Integrate SAP Fieldglass with your ATS to facilitate a smooth transition from candidate selection to contingent worker onboarding.

Ensure seamless transfer of candidate data, job offers, and onboarding requirements from the ATS to SAP Fieldglass.

Time and Attendance System Integration:

Integrate SAP Fieldglass with your organization's time and attendance system to accurately capture and track worker hours and attendance.

Automate the transfer of time and attendance data from the system to SAP Fieldglass for streamlined payroll processing and cost allocation.

Learning Management System (LMS) Integration:

Connect SAP Fieldglass with your organization's LMS to ensure seamless training and certification management for contingent workers.

Automatically assign and track training requirements within SAP Fieldglass based on worker profiles and job roles.

Performance Management System Integration:

Integrate SAP Fieldglass with your performance management system to capture and evaluate contingent worker performance.

Facilitate the transfer of performance evaluation data from SAP Fieldglass to the performance management system for comprehensive workforce performance analysis.

Section 3: Best Practices for Seamless Data Exchange

To ensure a successful integration between SAP Fieldglass and other systems, consider the following best practices:

Requirements Analysis:

Conduct a thorough analysis of integration requirements, including data exchange needs, system compatibility, and business process alignment.

System Configuration:

Configure SAP Fieldglass and other systems according to the integration requirements, ensuring that data formats, mappings, and security protocols are aligned.

Data Mapping and Transformation:

Define clear data mapping and transformation rules to ensure data consistency and accuracy between systems.

Consider data validation, field mapping, and any necessary data transformations during the integration process.

Testing and Validation:

Perform comprehensive testing of the integration to identify and resolve any issues or data discrepancies.

Validate data flow, synchronization, and system behavior to ensure seamless exchange of information.

Ongoing Monitoring and Maintenance:

Establish a monitoring mechanism to ensure the ongoing integrity and performance of the integration.

Regularly review and update integration configurations as needed, taking into account any system or process changes.

By exploring integration options with ERP systems, integrating with other HR and workforce management tools, and following best practices for seamless data exchange, you can create a connected ecosystem that maximizes the efficiency and effectiveness of your workforce management processes.

In the next chapter, we will explore advanced features and tips for optimizing your usage of SAP Fieldglass, enhancing automation, and improving overall performance.

Chapter 9: Advanced Features and Tips

Welcome to Chapter 9 of "Mastering SAP Fieldglass: A Comprehensive Guide to Streamlining Workforce Management." In this chapter, we will explore advanced features and provide tips to optimize your usage of SAP Fieldglass. By leveraging these advanced capabilities and following best practices, you can enhance automation, improve performance, and further streamline your workforce management processes.

Section 1: Leveraging Advanced Features and Functionalities

SAP Fieldglass offers a range of advanced features and functionalities that can enhance your workforce management experience. Here are some key areas to explore:

Workflow Automation:

Automate workflow processes, such as requisition approvals, vendor onboarding, or invoice processing, to reduce manual effort and improve efficiency.

Utilize workflow triggers, condition-based actions, and escalations to ensure timely processing and minimize delays.

Self-Service Portals:

Enable self-service portals for vendors, suppliers, and contingent workers to access and update their information, submit timesheets, or view payment details.

Empower stakeholders to perform necessary tasks and reduce administrative burden.

Advanced Analytics and Predictive Insights:

Explore advanced analytics features within SAP Fieldglass to gain deeper insights into your workforce data.

Utilize predictive analytics capabilities to forecast future workforce needs, cost trends, or compliance risks.

Mobile Access and Field Service Management:

Leverage SAP Fieldglass mobile applications to enable on-the-go access and facilitate field service management.

Empower contingent workers to access work orders, update deliverable statuses, and capture expenses directly from their mobile devices.

Section 2: Streamlining Processes through Automation and Workflow Enhancements

Automation and workflow enhancements can significantly improve the efficiency and accuracy of your workforce management processes. Consider the following tips to streamline your processes:

Process Mapping and Optimization:

Analyze your current processes and identify areas that can benefit from automation or workflow enhancements.

Map out the optimized processes, incorporating automation triggers, approval workflows, and system integration points.

Integration with Third-Party Systems:

Integrate SAP Fieldglass with other third-party systems, such as time and attendance systems or financial management platforms, to automate data exchange and eliminate manual data entry.

Alerts and Notifications:

Configure automated alerts and notifications within SAP Fieldglass to keep stakeholders informed about critical events or pending actions.

Ensure that relevant parties receive notifications for activities requiring their attention, such as pending approvals or upcoming deliverable deadlines.

Continuous Process Improvement:

Regularly review and analyze your workforce management processes to identify areas for further improvement.

Leverage feedback from stakeholders, monitor key metrics, and implement iterative enhancements to optimize your processes.

Section 3: Tips for Optimizing SAP Fieldglass Performance and User Experience

Optimizing performance and enhancing user experience are key to maximizing the benefits of SAP Fieldglass. Consider the following tips:

User Training and Support:

Provide comprehensive training to users, including administrators, managers, and contingent workers, to ensure they are proficient in using SAP Fieldglass.

Offer ongoing support and resources to address any questions or challenges that users may encounter.

Data Cleansing and Maintenance:

Regularly review and clean up data within SAP Fieldglass to ensure data accuracy and system performance.

Establish data governance practices to maintain data integrity and enforce data quality standards.

Regular System Updates and Patches:

Stay up to date with SAP Fieldglass updates and patches to benefit from the latest features, enhancements, and bug fixes.

Follow recommended best practices for system updates, including testing in a non-production environment before deploying to production.

User Interface Customization:

Customize the user interface of SAP Fieldglass to align with your organization's branding and user preferences.

Simplify navigation and streamline access to frequently used features or reports.

By leveraging advanced features and functionalities, streamlining processes through automation, and optimizing SAP Fieldglass performance and user experience, you can fully harness the potential of the platform and achieve greater efficiency in your workforce management practices.

Congratulations! You have reached the end of "Mastering SAP Fieldglass: A Comprehensive Guide to Streamlining Workforce Management." We hope this book has provided you with valuable insights and practical knowledge to effectively utilize SAP Fieldglass in your organization. Remember to continuously explore new features, stay updated with the latest releases, and adapt your processes to evolving business needs.

www.ingramcontent.com/pod-product-compliance
Lightning Source LLC
LaVergne TN
LVHW051620050326
832903LV00033B/4583